Pembroke, Cardigan & Montgomery's
by Peter Dale

Locomotive No. ... goods service to Lampeter at Aberayron Station, 7 July 1958.

ISBN 9781840334012

Printed by
St Edmundsbury Press
Bury St Edmunds, IP33 3TZ
Tel: 01284 701121

The publishers regret that they cannot supply copies of any pictures
featured in this book.

Glogue Station, looking towards Cardigan, 8 July 1958.

The publishers wish to thank the following for contributing photographs to this book: John Alsop for the front cover, pages 3-5, 9-14, 16, 17, 24-26, 29, 32, 35, 36, 38, 39, 41-45, 47 and the back cover; and Richard Casserley for pages 1, 2, 6-8, 15, 18, 19 (both), 20-23, 27, 28, 31, 33, 34, 37, 40, 46, 48 and the inside back cover.

INTRODUCTION

The former counties of Pembrokeshire, Cardiganshire and Montgomeryshire are now parts of the modern counties of Dyfed and Powys. During the nineteenth century west Wales remained relatively undeveloped. This was at least partly due to the late development of railways in the area, although there were many railway schemes, some more practical than others. Today, many areas of west Wales are again without rail links - even the county towns of two of the former counties, Montgomery and Cardigan, are without stations.

In railway terms, the area was dominated by two companies - the Great Western Railway, which was the largest of the pre-Grouping companies in mileage terms (at 3,005 miles); and the Cambrian Railways (don't forget the 's' – the Cambrian never did!), which was the seventeenth largest company in Britain. The Cambrian was formed on 25 July 1864 by the amalgamation of four companies - the Oswestry & Newtown, the Llanidloes & Newtown, the Newtown & Machynlleth and the Oswestry, Ellesmere & Welshpool railways. It grew by further amalgamations to a route mileage of 296 by 1921. It saw some interesting services as both the Great Western Railway and the London & North Western Railway ran services to Aberystwyth from London (Paddington and Euston respectively; some services were only through carriages). There was also an overnight service with coaches from both Euston and Paddington, arriving at Aberystwyth at 6.20 a.m. The Great Central ran trains there from Liverpool although they seemed to stop everywhere, taking five to six hours, and the Cheshire Lines Committee ran its trains from Manchester.

As the Grouping has already been mentioned perhaps some explanation for non-railway enthusiasts would be appropriate. Many of the railways in Britain were built by small companies, sometimes with the backing of a larger company. In the years leading up to 1923 there was a process of consolidation by which smaller companies amalgamated or were absorbed by larger ones, but in 1922 there were still well over 100 different railway companies in Britain. In 1923 all but a few minor companies were grouped into four larger concerns by Act of Parliament. They were the Great Western Railway (which continued in an enlarged form, including the Cambrian), the Southern Railway, the London Midland & Scottish Railway (which included the London & North Western Railway) and the London & North Eastern Railway. These four companies – often referred to as the 'Big Four' - continued until nationalisation in 1948.

Under British Railways a Modernisation Plan introduced in 1955 spelt the beginning of the end for steam on British Railways, while the Beeching Plan of 1963 saw the start of widespread closures of many minor, and some major, lines.

It is hoped these pictures will revive memories for older readers and evoke thoughts of a slower, perhaps more relaxed, age for younger ones – of a time when the railway station was the natural starting point for any journey that could not be accomplished by walking. There are some steam railways within the area well worth a visit, including the Welshpool & Llanfair, the Vale of Rheidol and the Teifi Valley railways.

Llanfechain Station.

Aberayron Branch

Passenger service withdrawn	7 May 1951	*Stations closed*	*Date*
Distance	12.2 miles	Felin Fach *	7 May 1951
Company	Lampeter, Aberayron & New Quay Light Railway	Ciliau-Aeron Halt	7 May 1951
		Crossways Halt	7 May 1951
Stations closed	*Date*	Llanerch-Ayron Halt	7 May 1951
Silian Halt	7 May 1951	Aberayron	7 May 1951
Blaenplwyf Halt	7 May 1951		
Talsarn Halt	7 May 1951	* Known as Ystrad until 1 January 1913.	

Talsarn Station.

Ystrad Station, later renamed Felin Fach.

There had been a number of proposals for a railway to Aberayron. One was for a 2 ft gauge line from Newcastle Emlyn to Aberayron and New Quay. In August 1898 another proposal for a 2 ft gauge line resulted in the Aberayron Extension Order being granted to the Vale of Rheidol Railway for a line from Aberystwyth, which would have made an interesting narrow gauge system. A Light Railway Order was granted in October 1906 for a line from a junction north of Lampeter (on the former Manchester & Milford line), despite opposition from the Cambrian Railways which supported a scheme for a line to Aberayron from Llanrhystyd Road Station, just east of Aberystwyth.

Construction commenced in October 1908 and the line opened to Aberayron for goods on 10 April 1911 and for passengers on 12 May. The line was worked by the Great Western from the outset, although it insisted that some curves be eased before commencing working. The company retained its independence until 1923 when it officially became part of the Great Western. Prior to the opening of the line the Great Western had started a bus service from Lampeter to Aberayron, and this was later followed by a service from Aberystwyth to Aberayron. However, it was reported that the railway reduced the cost of bringing coal from Lampeter to Aberayron from 10s (50p) to 2s 4d (about 12p) per ton. Services were provided by 0-4-2Ts with an autocoach.

Ciliau-Aeron Halt, looking towards Lampeter, 7 July 1958.

In 1933 there were four trains each way daily. By 1938 there was an additional service at 4.55 p.m. from Aberayron as far as Felin Fach and return, apparently for school transport as the timetable note says 'Saturdays and school holidays excepted'.

Passenger services ceased on 12 February 1951, but the line was not officially closed until 7 May of that year. Goods traffic lasted as far as Aberayron until 5 April 1965 and as far as Felin Fach until 1 October 1973.

Cardigan Branch *

Passenger service withdrawn	10 September 1962
Distance	25.2 miles (Cardigan Junction to Cardigan)
Company	Whitland & Taf Vale Railway / Whitland & Cardigan Railway

Stations closed	*Date*
Llanfyrnach	10 September 1962
Glogue	10 September 1962
Crymmych Arms	10 September 1962

Stations closed	*Date*
Boncath	10 September 1962
Kilgerran Halt **	10 September 1962
Cardigan ***	10 September 1962

* Closed stations on this line that were in Carmarthenshire were Llanfalteg, Login, Llanglydwen and Rhydowen.
** Known as Kilgerran until 10 September 1956.
*** Sometimes known as Cardigan for Gwbert-on-Sea.

Llanfyrnach Station, looking towards Whitland, 8 July 1957.

There were two schemes to provide a rail connection to Cardigan but the Carmarthen & Cardigan Railway's line eventually only got as far as Newcastle Emlyn (see the Newcastle Emlyn Branch section).

The Whitland & Taf Vale Railway was authorised on 12 July 1869 to build a line from a junction with the Great Western main line 2 miles west of Whitland to Glogue to serve quarries there. The line opened for goods on 24 March 1873 and was extended to Crymmych Arms in October 1874. Passenger services began on 12 July 1875. In August 1877 powers were obtained to extend the line to Cardigan and the name of the company was changed to the Whitland & Cardigan Railway at that time. The extension opened on 1 September 1886.

Kilgerran Station.

During construction talks had been going on with the Great Western, resulting in an agreement in 1883 for them to work the line once it opened to Cardigan. The original line, which had been built to light railway standards, was brought up to main line standards at the same time. The Great Western took over the local company in August 1890.

The Whitland & Cardigan had three locomotives, all built by Fox Walker of Bristol, which passed to the Great Western at the takeover. These engines subsequently had interesting careers. Numbers 1 and 2 were sold out of Great Western service – No. 1 ended its days on a colliery line in Durham in 1947, while No. 2 went to the East Kent Railway where it was scrapped in 1934. No. 3 survived into nationalisation and was withdrawn from Oswestry in January 1950.

Cardigan Station.

In later days the line was frequently the haunt of 45XX class tanks, although the first and last trains each day were worked by 19XX or 16XX pannier tanks. This was because these workings required the locomotive to be stabled overnight at Cardigan and the 45XX class was too heavy to cross the turntable which was in front of the engine shed.

In 1887 there were three through services daily, with an additional short working as far as Crymmych Arms. The third class fare was 2s 11d from Whitland to Cardigan (just under 15p) while the first class fare was 5s 10d (about 29p). In 1910 there were four daily return services and this service was largely unchanged for the rest of the line's life. After the line closed goods services lingered on until 27 May 1963.

Corris Railway *

Passenger service withdrawn	1 January 1931
Distance	6.5 miles (Machynlleth to Aberllefenni)
Company	Corris Machynlleth & River Dovey Tramroad

Stations closed	*Date*
Machynlleth	1 January 1931

* Closed stations on this line that were in Merioneth were Fridd Gate, Dolydderwen Crossing, Lliwdy, Llwyngwern, Escair-Geiliog, Corris, Garneddwen and Aberllefenni.

The Corris, Machynlleth & River Dovey Tramroad Company obtained an Act of Parliament in July 1858 and built a 2 ft 3 in. gauge horse-worked line (although loaded slate wagons could come down as far as Machynlleth by gravity) from Derwenglas, on the River Dovey, to slate quarries at Ratgoed. The original Act prohibited the company from using steam locomotives with a penalty of £100 per day they were used. The line opened in piecemeal fashion as construction proceeded and was open throughout by 1863. The section from Machynlleth to Derwenglas fell into disuse at an early date following the opening of the standard gauge line to Machynlleth which allowed slates to be transshipped there.

A further Act of July 1864 changed the name to the Corris Railway, permitted abandonment of the Derwenglas section and the use of steam locomotives. The line passed into control of the Bristol Tramways & Carriage Company in October 1887 and steam locomotives were introduced in 1879, followed by an official passenger service as far as Corris in July 1883 (passengers had been carried unofficially since 1874). The service was extended to Aberllefenni in August 1887. The line was unaffected by the Grouping (being owned by a tramway company) and only became part of the Great Western in August 1930 after Sir George White, who had a controlling interest in Bristol Tramways, died and his interest was sold to the Great Western. The Corris Railway competed with the Great Western bus service between Machynlleth and Aberllefenni, but lost and its passenger service was withdrawn after passenger numbers fell.

The line continued in use for mineral traffic and survived long enough to become part of British Railways. It closed in August 1948 when the River Dovey threatened to cut through the line after severe rain. The line's last two locomotives, Nos. 3 and 4, were bought by the Talyllyn Railway in March 1951, a line that is of the same gauge and was then in its early days as a preserved line. Part of the Corris Railway has now also reopened as a preserved line.

Machynlleth Station, *c.* **1912.**

Kerry Branch

Passenger service withdrawn	9 February 1931
Distance	3.8 miles
Company	Oswestry & Newtown Railway

Stations closed	*Date*
Fron Fraith Halt	9 February 1931
Goitre Halt	9 February 1931
Kerry	9 February 1931

The Kerry Branch was authorised as part of the Oswestry & Newtown Railway (which became a constituent of the Cambrian Railways in July 1864) by an Act of 17 May 1861. It opened for passenger traffic on 2 March 1863 and for goods on 1 July the same year. The line followed a tortuous path up the narrow, steep valley of the River Mule to a terminus about a mile from the village of Kerry.

In 1887 there were six trains each way daily, taking 20 minutes for the journey, although by 1910 the service had dropped to three each way, taking 25 minutes. By 1922 services had dwindled to two. After the Cambrian became part of the Great Western group the two halts were opened but this did not stop closure to passengers in 1931. Goods traffic continued until May 1956.

Kerry Station, 1904.

The train was known as the 'Kerry Express' and ran as a mixed train. In the early 1900s the single coach provided one first class and three third class compartments, while the regular power was one of three 0-4-0STs built by Sharp Stewart in 1863. After these locomotives were withdrawn in 1907 three 0-6-0Ts bought from the Lambourn Valley Railway took over. These were followed by a variety of tank locomotives, Dean Goods 0-6-0s, and even a 4-4-0 passenger locomotive ventured up the line.

A 2 ft gauge tramway was built from Kerry Station to the Bryn-Llywarch estate around 1887; it carried timber and stone slabs until 1895 when it was lifted. In 1917 the Forestry Commission laid a line of the same gauge over the route and it was worked, at first, by German prisoners of war. Later, it was worked by a contractor until traffic ceased in the early 1920s.

Llanfyllin Branch *

Passenger service withdrawn	18 January 1965	Stations closed	*Date*
Distance	8.8 miles (Llanymynech to Llanfyllin)	Llansantffraid	18 January 1965
Company	Tanat Valley Railway		

Stations closed	*Date*
Llanfyllin	18 January 1965
Bryngwyn Halt **	18 January 1965
Llanfechain	18 January 1965

* The closed station on this line that was in Shropshire was Carreghofa Halt.

** Originally known as Brongwyn, then Bryngwyn, before becoming Bryngwyn Halt in 1923.

Llanfyllin Station, 28 May 1932.

The Llanfyllin Branch was built under powers that had been granted to the Oswestry & Newtown Railway in May 1861. The line was inspected in June 1863 and opened on 17 July that year when a seaside excursion train of 23 coaches was run to Borth. Regular service trains ran to and from Oswestry. During the 1880s the line saw heavy traffic in conjunction with the construction of the Vyrnwy Reservoir. As plans to extend the branch to the construction site were considered impractical materials had to be taken by road from Llanfyllin using teams of horses.

Bryngwyn Station.

In 1887 there were six trains in each direction daily and there was a signal at Bryngwyn that intending passengers could operate to warn the driver to stop. The number of trains had reduced to five by 1910, although there was an extra train on Wednesdays. The basic pattern was maintained with extra trains on Wednesdays and, later, Saturdays. In its early days the line was worked by 2-4-0Ts and 0-4-4Ts and, later, by Great Western pannier tanks.

Llansantffraid, looking towards Llanfyllin, 14 September 1956.

Maenclochog Railway

Passenger service withdrawn	25 October 1937	*Stations closed*	*Date*
Distance	23.3 miles	Puncheston *	25 October 1937
Company	Narberth Road & Maenclochog Railway /	New Inn Bridge Halt	25 October 1937
	North Pembrokeshire & Fishguard Railway	Rosebush **	25 October 1937
		Maenclochog **	25 October 1937
Stations closed	*Date*	Llanycefn **	25 October 1937
Letterston *	25 October 1937		
Beulah Halt	25 October 1937	* Closed between 8 January 1917 and 14 November 1921.
Martell Bridge Halt	25 October 1937	** Closed January 1883, reopened 11 April 1895; closed again between 8
Castlebythe Halt	25 October 1937	January 1917 and 12 July 1920.

This line was built by a Mr Cropper from his slate quarries at Rosebush to a junction with the Great Western Railway at Clynderwen (known as Narberth Road until 1 December 1875) under a Board of Trade Certificate of June 1872 (few lines were built under this form of authority, which existed as a result of the Railway Construction Facilities Act of 1864 and could only be used in cases where there was no opposition to a line and all the landowners concerned consented). It opened for passengers on 19 September 1876 and an attempt was made to develop Rosebush as a holiday resort. The line was the steepest standard gauge passenger line in Britain with a gradient of 1 in 27 for about 1.9 miles (a distinction shared with the Middleton Junction and Oldham branch of the London, Midland & Scottish Railway).

On 8 August 1878 the Rosebush & Fishguard Railway was authorised to extend the line from Rosebush to Goodwick, near Fishguard. It bought the Maenclochog line and began work on the extension but got into financial difficulties and the existing line closed on 1 January 1883. The name of the line was changed to the North Pembrokeshire & Fishguard Railway in August 1884.

Letterston Station, *c.* **1906.**

An auto train at Rosebush Station.

In 1892 Joseph Rowlands, a Birmingham solicitor, took control of the North Pembrokeshire and also bought the Rosslare Harbour works in Ireland. The North Pembrokeshire was reconditioned and reopened, with a 9-mile extension to Letterston, opening for passengers on 11 April 1895. In 1893 an Act had been passed authorising the Fishguard Bay Railway and Pier Company to build a connecting line to Letterston and a pier at Fishguard. Rowlands then approached the Great Western with the intention of selling these lines to that company. When the Great Western showed no interest he promoted a line from Beag, just north of Clynderwen, by a very roundabout route that passed near Pendine on the coast to join the London & North Western at Abergwili near Carmarthen. Whether such an indirect route would have had much practical use is debatable but the bill passed through Parliament in 1895. At this point the Great Western decided it did not want to see the London & North Western controlling both routes to Ireland (it already owned the main line to Holyhead) and, bearing in mind that the original intention of the South Wales Railway had been a terminus at Fishguard, the Great Western acquired the North Pembrokeshire in February 1898. The extension to Fishguard and Goodwick opened on 1 July 1899. The steep gradient involved made it impractical as a through route and the Great Western built a new line, extending the existing main line beyond Clarbeston Road, which opened on 30 August 1906.

Services ran between Clynderwen and Fishguard with three trains a day in 1910. The line was closed on 8 January 1917 but reopened, after the war, in stages. In 1922 there were three return trains per day between Clynderwen and Puncheston and three between Letterston and Fishguard. Through services did not resume until 9 July 1923. The four halts on the line were opened between 1928 and 1930 in an effort to boost traffic. Latterly trains were auto trains worked by 48XX series tanks and there were three trains daily from Clynderwen to Fishguard. It was at first intended to close the line from September 1937 but closure was delayed until the following month.

Manchester & Milford Railway *

Passenger service withdrawn	14 December 1964 (Strata Florida to Aberystwyth) / 22 February 1965 (Carmarthen to Strata Florida)
Distance	41.3 miles (Pencader Junction to Aberystwyth)
Company	Manchester & Milford Railway.

Stations closed	*Date*
Lampeter	22 February 1965
Derry Ormond **	22 February 1965
Llangybi	22 February 1965
Olmarch Halt	22 February 1965
Pont Llanio	22 February 1965
Tregaron	22 February 1965

Stations closed	*Date*
Alltddu Halt	22 February 1965
Strata Florida	22 February 1965
Caradog Falls Halt	14 December 1964
Trawscoed	14 December 1964
Felindyffryn Halt	14 December 1964
Llanilar	14 December 1964
Llanrhystyd Road	14 December 1964

* The closed stations on this line that were in Carmarthenshire were Pencader Junction, Bryn Teifi, Maesycrugiau, Llanbyther and Pencarreg Halt.

** Known as Bettws until July 1874.

Lampeter Station, looking towards Carmarthen, 7 July 1958.

Locomotive No. 80104 with the 1035 service from Carmarthen at Tregaron Station, 17 June 1963.

The Manchester & Milford Railway was part of the Great Western's route from Carmarthen to Aberystwyth. Its origins lay in a scheme, thought up during the Railway Mania of 1845, to link the towns in its title so that products from Manchester could access the port at Milford.

By 1860 the proposal was for a line from Llanidloes, on the Mid Wales Railway, via Lampeter to a junction with the Carmarthen & Cardigan Railway at Pencader. Connections north of Llanidloes and south of Pencader were to be achieved by running powers over the railways concerned, including the laying of a third rail on broad gauge lines to the south. When an Act for this was passed in July 1860 provision was also made for a branch from Devil's Bridge to Aberystwyth. The first 2 miles from Llanidloes, as far as Penpontbren, coincided with a line proposed by the Mid Wales to Newbridge-on-Wye; beyond there the Manchester & Milford built their own line as far as Llangurig, a distance of 3 miles, and it only wanted Board of Trade approval to open. However the rest of the line as authorised included expensive engineering works in the shape of a 280 ft high viaduct and tunnels of about 1 mile and the company intended applying for powers for another, shorter line. Further proposals failed to make any progress.

Locomotive No. 7826 at Alltddu Halt with the 1155 service from Aberystwyth to Carmarthen, 17 June 1963.

Despite being chronically short of money construction began on the line north of Pencader which opened to Lampeter on 1 January 1866 and to Strata Florida on 1 September 1866. On opening, the company published a timetable showing a through service from Manchester to Milford that involved two overnight stops and a horse-drawn coach service! The year before the company had obtained powers for a line from Strata Florida to Aberystwyth and this opened on 12 August 1867.

Strata Florida, looking towards Aberystwyth, 26 August 1948.

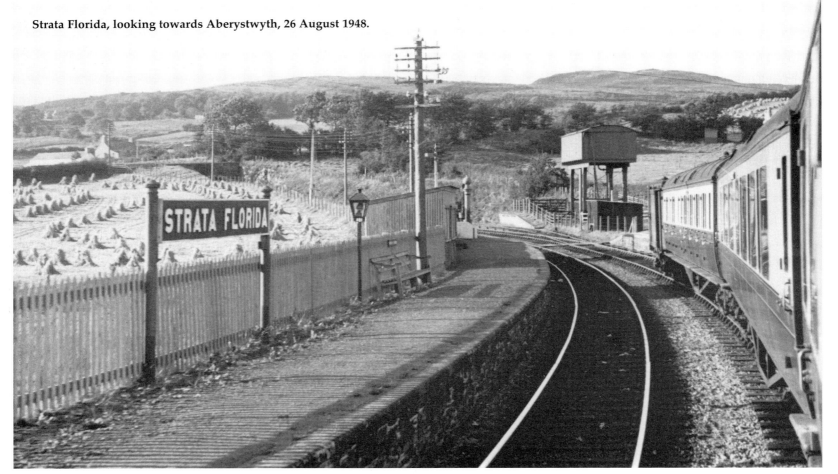

Manchester & Milford Railway

Thus this grand scheme to link two places 170 miles apart became a local line of only 41 miles and the only running powers it had was by means of a third rail over the Carmarthen & Cardigan to Carmarthen. Manchester & Milford passenger trains only ran to Carmarthen from 1 November 1866 to July 1872, after which time passengers had to change at Pencader. The line went into receivership in 1880 and was leased by the Great Western in 1906, in the face of fierce opposition from the Cambrian. It was absorbed by the Great Western in 1911 but until then the Manchester & Milford ran its own services and in 1906 had 8 locomotives. One of these, No. 2 'Carmarthen', a Sharp Stewart 2-4-0, came to an unusual end when its boiler exploded at Maesycrugiau on 19 August 1890. No one was injured but the steam dome is probably still in the River Teify.

In 1887, as the Carmarthen & Cardigan and Manchester & Milford were separate, trains from Carmarthen ran to Llandyssil and passengers for Aberystwyth had to change at Pencader. By 1910 the whole line was run by the Great Western and trains ran through from Carmarthen to Aberystwyth, there being five trains daily in each direction except on Sundays. By 1961 the service was down to three trains daily in each direction plus an early morning (6.10 a.m.) Carmarthen departure arriving in Aberystwyth at 8.43 a.m. It is this last train which provided the author's only experience of the line, while making a first trip to see the Welsh narrow gauge lines in September 1964.

Llanrhystyd Road, looking towards Carmarthen, 18 June 1963.

Mawddy Railway *

Passenger service withdrawn	1 January 1931
Distance	6.8 miles
Company	Mawddy Railway

Stations closed	*Date*
Cemmaes **	1 January 1931
Aberangell ***	1 January 1931

* Closed stations on this line that were in Merionethshire were Mallwyd and Dinas Mawddwy.
** Known as Cemmes until it closed on 17 April 1901; named Cemmaes upon reopening on 31 July 1911.
*** Closed 17 April 1901 and reopened 31 July 1911.

The Mawddwy Railway obtained its Act (as the Mowddwy Railway) in July 1865 to provide an outlet for the agricultural produce and slate of the area. The lightly laid line opened on 1 October 1867 from a junction with the Cambrian Railways at Cemmaes Road. Traffic did not reach the expected levels - in 1887 there were five passenger trains in each direction daily, all three classes being catered for. The line had two Manning Wardle 0-6-0STs, 'Disraeli' and 'Mawddwy' and a mixture of coaches, five of which were included in the sale catalogue in 1909. The line closed to passengers on 17 April 1901 and entirely in April 1908 without ever paying a dividend.

David Davies, the chairman of the Cambrian Railways, bought the line and a Light Railway Order was granted in March 1910. The line was rebuilt as a Light Railway by the Cambrian, which worked it on reopening in July 1911 in return for 70% of the receipts. On reopening there were 4 daily trains each way. 'Mawddwy' continued in service but 'Disraeli' was scrapped and additional motive power was provided by Cambrian tanks. The line became part of the Great Western at the Grouping. After passenger services ceased in 1931 goods traffic continued, often worked by Dean Goods locomotives. In 1950 the condition of the bridge over the River Dovey forced the suspension of services and the line closed officially on 1 July 1951.

At Aberangell there was an interchange facility with the Hendre-ddu Tramway which opened a little after the Mawddwy Railway to a gauge of about 1 ft 11 in. It ran about 5 miles to the west serving, with branches, various slate quarries. It was privately owned and charged tolls for other users. It was worked by gravity to Aberangell, horses being used to return the empty wagons. Later a Simplex locomotive was used; workmen also used various homemade contraptions some fitted with motors. It all came to an end during the Second World War.

Cemmaes during closure, 1904.

Mid Wales Line *

Passenger service withdrawn   31 December 1962
Distance   55.8 miles
Company Llanidloes & Newtown Railway (Moat Lane Junction–Llanidloes)/
Mid Wales Railway (Llanidloes–Talyllyn Junction)

Stations closed	*Date*
Moat Lane	3 January 1863
Llandinam	31 December1962
Dolwen Halt **	31 December1962
Llanidloes ***	31 December1962
Tylwch Halt ****	31 December1962

* The closed stations on this line that were in Radnorshire were Glan-Yr-Afon Halt, Pantydwr, St Harmons, Marteg Halt, Rhayader, Doldowlod, Newbridge-on-Wye, Builth Road, Builth Wells, Llanfaredd Halt, Aberedw, Tir Celyn Platform, Erwood, Llanstephan Halt, Boughrood & Llyswen, Three Cocks Junction, Talgarth, Trefeinon, Llangorse Lake Halt and Talyllyn.
** Known as Dolwen until 3 September 1956.
*** The first station here closed by January 1862, when it was replaced as the line was extended to the south.
**** Known as Tylwch until 10 July 1939.

Moat Lane, 24 August 1948. The Mid Wales line is on the left.

The Mid Wales Line was formed by two railways: the Llanidloes & Newtown Railway, opened to passengers in August 1859, and the Mid Wales Railway which was formed to build an extension southwards from Llanidloes.

Llanidloes Station.

The Llanidloes & Newtown Railway was promoted by interests in the town of Llanidloes fearful that other proposals would leave their town off the railway map. In the event their bill was passed on 4 August 1853, while the other proposals failed. Goods traffic started on 30 April 1859, but passenger services did not begin until 2 September that year. The first inspection by Colonel Yolland found the works incomplete and a second inspection was made by Captain Ross on 6 August. As the connecting line to the rest of the rail system, the Oswestry & Newtown, was not finished the rolling stock had to come by road from Oswestry – the Oswestry & Newtown opened in June 1861.

The Mid Wales Railway southwards was originally promoted as part of another scheme for a railway from Manchester to Milford, however only the northern section, as far as Newbridge-on-Wye, was authorised on 1 August 1859. The Mid Wales also promoted a line further south to join the Hereford Hay & Brecon at Three Cocks and this was authorised on 3 July 1860. There was a formal opening ceremony on 23 August 1864 and passenger services began throughout on 24 September.

Tylwch Station.

The Mid Wales was in financial difficulty from its opening and in 1866 services were cut and some stock was sold. A working agreement was reached with the Cambrian in 1888 and the Mid Wales was taken over by the Cambrian in June 1904.

For the opening Kitson supplied six 0-4-2s for passenger services and four 0-6-0s for goods. After 1888 Cambrian 2-4-0s and 0-6-0s worked the line. In Great Western days some 2-4-0 passenger locomotives could be seen but the line was long the haunt of Dean Goods 0-6-0 locomotives. In later British Railways days Type 2 Ivatt 2-6-0s were often seen.

Services on the line were never plentiful - three or four trains in each direction daily were the norm with an additional service south of Builth Road. In 1910 there was one service in each direction on a Sunday, but this had gone by 1922. An interesting service was the through train from South Wales to Aberystwyth. This began in 1880 with a through train from Cardiff. By 1922 the through service ran from Aberystwyth to Treherbert and Merthyr - useful but only if you wanted to travel on a Saturday or Monday. Some vestige of this continued until 1938 at least and at one time the Cambrian engine used to work through to Merthyr.

Newcastle Emlyn Branch *

Passenger service withdrawn	15 September 1952
Distance	10.5 miles
Company	Carmarthen & Cardigan Railway / Great Western Railway

Stations closed	*Date*
Henllan	15 September 1952

* The closed stations on this line that were in Carmarthenshire were Llandyssil, Pentrecourt Platform and Newcastle Emlyn.

Henllan Station.

The Carmarthen & Cardigan Railway was proposed in 1854 as a broad gauge line from a junction, near Carmarthen, with the South Wales Railway to Cardigan. After financial and construction problems the line opened as far as Llandyssil in June 1864. After the Great Western took over running, in August 1881, the Carmarthen to Aberystwyth service, on the section from Pencader to Llandyssil, was relegated to branch status. The Newcastle Emlyn extension was only built after the Great Western had taken over. It opened on 1 July 1895 but the extension to Cardigan was never built. In 1910 there were five return trains daily with an additional two as far as Llandyssil on Saturday, taking about half an hour for the journey. Part of the line is now open as the narrow gauge Teifi Valley Railway based around Henllan Station.

Neyland

Passenger service withdrawn	15 June 1964
Distance	4.3 miles
Company	South Wales Railway

Stations closed	*Date*
Neyland *	15 June 1964

* This station opened as Milford Haven but was renamed Neyland in February 1859. It was renamed New Milford in November 1859 and reverted back to Neyland on 1 September 1906

When the original proposals for the South Wales Railway were made in 1844 a line was not planned to Neyland at all. The western terminus of the South Wales Railway was intended to be at Fishguard, with a view to tapping Irish traffic to Wexford, only 54 miles across the water.

Initial progress was good and by August 1847 construction was in full swing, although a recession later that year forced a slowdown. The Great Famine in Ireland in 1849 caused great hardship and projects were scaled down accordingly. The Waterford, Wexford, Wicklow & Dublin Railway was cut down to become the Dublin & Wicklow Railway and it was clear that the hoped for Irish traffic would not be forthcoming. Work west of Clarbeston Road was abandoned and Fishguard did not get its railway for another half century. Parliamentary powers were obtained in 1852 to extend the proposed branch from Clarbeston Road to Haverfordwest as far as Milford Haven. The place chosen for the terminus was Neyland, on the Haven.

The line opened on 15 April 1856 as a broad gauge line, although it was narrowed in 1872. Just as some towns arose because of the canals, others arose because of the railway and that is what happened at Neyland. In 1851 the village had a population of less than 200 but by the 1861 Census this had grown to 1,045. The South Wales Hotel opened in 1858 and there were many new houses, shops and chapels built. Wharves were built for the steamers to Ireland, services having begun in August 1856 to Waterford and later Cork. For a little while a Portuguese company operated a monthly service to Portugal and on to Brazil, but after a few months it diverted to Liverpool.

In 1865 there were four trains each way, two of which originated in Paddington. A first class single cost 49s 6d (about £2.48) while a third class ticket cost 23s 9d (about £1.19) for the 285 miles at the Parliamentary rate of 1d per mile. There was a steamer connection to Waterford for trains arriving at 6.50 p.m. In 1887 there were eight daily arrivals, of which five started at Paddington, with a daily steamer to Waterford and to Passage (for Cork) three times per week. By 1910 the situation had changed as, following the opening of the line to Fishguard, most passengers had to change at Clarbeston Road. There were eight daily arrivals of which only two came from Paddington, but on Saturday evenings there was a sleeping car from Paddington due at 6.40 a.m. although there were no steamer connections.

In September 1863 the Milford Railway opened from a junction on the South Wales main line (as it was then) at Johnston. It was initially worked as a branch but as the town of Old Milford (Milford Haven) grew in importance some trains worked through and passengers for Neyland had to change at Johnston, although there were still through carriages to Neyland from Paddington twice daily. Closure came about under the Beeching plan and although there is still a railway to Milford Haven it is to the town of Old Milford, while Neyland is left to dream of its former importance as part of a through route to Ireland.

The 0705 service from Johnstone arriving at Neyland Station, 7 July 1958.

Welshpool to Oswestry *

Passenger service withdrawn	18 January 1965
Distance	15.8 miles
Company	Oswestry & Newtown Railway

Stations closed	*Date*
Buttington **	12 September 1960
Pool Quay	18 January 1965
Arddleen Halt ***	18 January 1965
Four Crosses	18 January 1965

* The closed stations on this line that were in Shropshire were Llanymynech, Pant, Llynclys and Oswestry.
** Originally known as Cefn Junction.
*** Known as Arddleen until 14 January 1964.

The Welshpool to Oswestry section of the Cambrian was built by the Oswestry & Newtown Railway which was authorised on 26 June 1855. The Oswestry to Pool Quay section was inspected by Colonel Yolland in April 1860 and opened on 1 May 1860, followed by the section into Welshpool on 14 August. Although built as a single track line land was purchased to allow for later doubling, although the line remained single with passing loops. The remainder of the line to Newtown (where there was a joint station with the Llanidloes & Newtown) opened in June the following year and most trains ran to Llanidloes. There were seven trains daily over the section in 1887. Various Cambrian locos were used on the line and in Great Western days Moguls and Bulldogs could be seen but the axle loading remained restricted so that the crack 'Cambrian Coast Express' was hauled by a Manor class 4-6-0 from Shrewsbury to Aberystwyth.

The Shrewsbury & Welshpool Railway opened to a junction with the Oswestry & Newtown at Buttington in 1862. For many years there were two separate single tracks into Welshpool - a connection was only put in between the lines at Buttington in 1893. The section from Welshpool to Buttington remains open as part of the link southwards to Aberystwyth.

Pool Quay, looking towards Oswestry, 28 August 1964.

Four Crosses Station, c. 1905.

Four Crosses (Mont.) Railway Station.

Plynlimon & Hafan Tramway

Passenger service withdrawn	16 August 1898
Distance	7.3 miles
Company	Plynlimon & Hafan Company

Stations closed	*Date*
Llanfihangel	16 August 1898
Talybont	16 August 1898

This short - and short-lived - line was built to provide a way of shipping the ore from the lead mines above Talybont. It was also known as the Hafan & Talybont tramway or the Hafan Tram. The original intention was to take the line to the coast but the Cambrian would not permit it to cross its line. It was then proposed to take the line to a leet where the ore could be loaded on ships that would then sail under the Cambrian line. After this idea was abandoned another route was suggested to connect Llanfihangel with Talybont. After some discussion, agreement was reached with Sir Lewis Pryse, who owned most of the land in the area, for a line running to an interchange siding with the Cambrian on the east side of Llanfihangel Station. As the line was being built without authorisation of Parliament (and so without compulsory purchase powers) this agreement was vital.

Construction began in January 1896 to a gauge of 2 ft 3 in. The Plynlimon & Hafan Company was formed in October 1896 to take over the quarries and railway. There were early hopes that the traffic would warrant conversion to standard gauge with passenger traffic as far as Talybont. There was a delay getting the track materials but then the line was completed very quickly, being finished by the beginning of April 1897. One coach had been ordered but, due to the poor state of the track between Llanfihangel and Talybont (there had already been two fatal accidents on the line), the passenger service between those places did not begin until 28 March 1898. The service was Mondays only and lasted only until 16 August 1898. The line continued to carry mineral traffic until sometime in the summer of 1899 when traffic ceased and the Hafan company went into liquidation in December 1899.

The line had some interesting locomotives such as 'Victoria', a vertical boiler tram locomotive built by Slee and Co. of Warrington. John Slee was a director of the tram company and this locomotive was the only one Slee built. It was not very successful, often being short of steam, and its fate is unknown. The company also had a 2-4-0T, built by Bagnall for a Brazilian sugar plantation although it was sold to the Hafan company instead and named 'Talybont'. After the line closed it was sold to the Vale of Rheidol company at Aberystwyth where it was regauged to 1 ft 11½ in. and named 'Rheidol'. It lasted until 1924 when it was scrapped at Swindon, the Great Western having taken over the Vale of Rheidol at the Grouping.

Tanat Valley Light Railway *

Passenger service withdrawn	15 January 1951
Distance	14.8 miles (Porthywaen to Llangynog)
Company	Tanat Valley Railway

Stations closed	*Date*
Llangynog	15 January 1951
Penybontfawr	15 January 1951
Pedair-Ffordd	15 January 1951

* The closed stations on this line that were in Denbeighshire were Llanrhaiadr Mochnant, Pentrefelin, Llangedwyn and Llansilin Road. The closed stations in Shropshire were Llanyblodwell, Blodwell Junction and Pontywaen.

There had been a number of schemes to connect Llangynog with the railway system. Some of these would have placed it on grandiose trunk lines to link the Midlands with the Welsh Coast while another planned a narrow gauge line from Welshpool via Llanfair Caerinion. The passing of the Light Railways Act in 1896 was the stimulus for two new schemes: a 2 ft 6 in. gauge line from Llanfyllin and a standard gauge line from Porthywaen (some 3 miles south of Oswestry). The Light Railway Commissioners approved the latter scheme and a Light Railway Order was granted on 4 January 1899. The line was effectively in two sections: from Llangynog to the Nantmawr branch of the old Potteries, Shrewsbury and North Wales Railway (the 'Potts') at Blodwell Junction, which the Cambrian had been working for mineral traffic since 1898. After a quarter of a mile it resumed its own right of way for 1 mile to a junction with the Porthywaen branch of the Cambrian.

After some financial difficulties the line opened on 6 January 1904 and was worked by the Cambrian (before the official opening Free Market Day specials had been run by the contractor). The four daily trains ran as mixed trains to and from Oswestry. There was also a service from Blodwell Junction to Llanymynech twice daily, although this stopped in 1917. Only four months after the opening a receiver was appointed. In March 1921 the line was taken over by the Cambrian and so became part of the Great Western. There was almost twenty times more mineral traffic than passenger and by 1922 there were only three passenger trains daily.

After passenger services were withdrawn, goods traffic continued as far as Llanrhaiadr Mochnant until 1960 and from Blodwell Quarries until October 1988. In Cambrian days the line was worked by Sharp Stewart 2-4-0Ts or the ex-Lambourn Valley 0-6-0Ts. Various Great Western types worked the line, including the ex-Liskeard & Looe Railway 'Lady Margaret' and Bristol & Exeter 0-6-0T No. 1376.

Great Western 2-4-0T locomotive No. 1197 (an ex-Cambrian), at the shed site at Llangynog Station.

Penybontfawr Station.

Van Railway

Passenger service withdrawn	July 1879	*Stations closed*	*Date*
Distance	6.3 miles	Pwll Glas *	July 1879
Company	Van Railway	Red House	July 1879
		Caersws	July 1879
Stations closed	*Date*		
Garth & Van Road	July 1879	* This station was originally known as Trefeglwys.	
Cerist	July 1879		

Caersws Station, 1948.

The Van Railway Company was registered in June 1870 and the line opened from a junction with the Cambrian at Caersws (where the Van Railway had its own station) for mineral and freight traffic on 14 August 1871. The *raison d'être* of the line was the lead and silver mines at Van. There was a boom in the shares, which had a nominal value of £4 10s, but were traded at £86 at which level they were greatly overvalued and the bubble was soon pricked. However, the mines were very productive for about 12 years, employing up to 150 men and producing as much as 600 tons of lead per month. They suffered from foreign competition - in particular from Spanish mines which produced ore with a higher silver content - and closed in the early 1890s.

A Board of Trade Certificate was issued under the Railway Construction Facilities Act on 22 May 1873 when it was decided the line could carry passengers. On 1 December 1873 a twice-daily passenger service began, using two second-hand Midland coaches, as far as Garth & Van Road, although the line ran another third of a mile to Van Mines. John Ceiriog Hughes, a well-known Welsh poet, was General Manager of the line for a while and some of the passenger traffic was a result of people coming to talk to him. After the passenger service ceased freight traffic continued until 1893. However, the line reopened in August 1896 and was worked by the Cambrian as it wanted a source of good ballast. The company remained independent until the Grouping when it became part of the Great Western. Occasional freight trains were worked until 4 November 1940 when it finally closed. The Van Railway worked the line with a pair of Manning Wardle 0-6-0STs which later went to the Cambrian. Later, ex-Lambourn Valley 0-6-0Ts were to be seen on the line.

Welshpool & Llanfair Light Railway

Passenger service withdrawn	9 February 1931
Distance	9.1 miles
Company	Welshpool & Llanfair Light Railway

Stations closed	*Date*
Welshpool Seven Stars	9 February 1931
Welshpool Raven Square *	9 February 1931
Golfa	9 February 1931
Sylfaen Halt **	9 February 1931
Castle Caereinion	9 February 1931

Stations closed	*Date*
Dolarddyn Crossing Halt	9 February 1931
Cyfronydd	9 February 1931
Heniarth ***	9 February 1931
Llanfair Caereinion	9 February 1931

* The present Raven Square Station is to the west of the original one.
** Known as Sylfaen Farm Siding until 1 February 1913.
*** Known as Heniarth Gate until 1 February 1913.

Welshpool Raven Square.

Sylfaen Halt, 1943.

There had been a number of schemes to link Llanfair to the railway network. An early narrow gauge scheme failed after opposition from the Earl of Powis, although a successor lent support to the successful scheme. Other schemes to both standard gauge and 3 ft gauge were proposed but it was not until the Light Railways Act was passed that real progress was made. In September 1899 a Light Railway Order was granted to build a 2 ft 6 in. gauge line from a junction with the Cambrian at Welshpool to Llanfair. The Welshpool & Llanfair differed from other narrow gauge railways in Wales that were built mainly for a specific mineral traffic (with other traffic materialising later) as it was a true secondary line and had the advantage that it did not have to build to a gauge already determined by the industries it was to serve – thus, the somewhat unusual gauge (at least in Britain) was chosen.

Cyfronydd.

When the Montgomeryshire Canal opened it was granted powers to build feeder tramroads to bring traffic to the canal and one of these served the Stondart Quarry at Welshpool. It had fallen into disuse by 1854 but the right of way still existed and was incorporated into the Welshpool & Llanfair. By the time the line opened in 1903 expenses had doubled to £47,000 per mile and some economies were made including the provision of only two locomotives instead of the planned three. The line opened for goods traffic on 9 March 1903 and for passengers on 4 April. It was worked by the Cambrian, which received 60% of gross receipts. Goods traffic consisted of sheep, timber, coal etc. In 1910 the passenger service was four trains to Llanfair but only three return. The company remained independent until the Grouping when it became part of the Great Western. From 1925 that company placed a bus service in competition with the trains and passenger traffic fell sharply so that passenger services ceased on 9 February 1931. Goods traffic continued until 31 October 1956. A final Stephenson Locomotive Society Special ran on 3 November that year.

Locomotive No. 822 with the 2.25 p.m. service from Llanfair at Castle Caereinion, 24 August 1948.

Happily, this was not the end of the line and a preservation scheme has reopened the line from Llanfair to a new station at Welshpool Raven Square. The original locomotives have been joined by others from different parts of the world. However, unlike some preserved lines, the Welshpool & Llanfair has kept a lot of its light railway atmosphere and, at least on weekdays, trains still amble along the meandering route much as they would have done 100 years ago. Well worth a visit for anyone in the area.

CLOSED PASSENGER STATIONS ON LINES STILL OPEN TO PASSENGERS
Cambrian main line (Welshpool to Aberystwyth)

Stations closed	Date
Welshpool *	18 May 1992
Cilcewydd East **	27 February 1994
Cilcewydd West **	27 February 1994
Forden	14 June 1965
Montgomery	14 June 1965
Abermule	14 June 1965
Newtown ***	10 June 1861
Scafell Halt ****	7 March 1955
Moat Lane Junction †	31 December 1962
Pontdolgoch	14 June 1965
Carno	14 June 1965
Talerddig	14 June 1965
Llanbrynmair	14 June 1965
Commins Coch Halt	14 June 1965
Cemmes Road	14 June 1965
Glandyfi ††	14 June 1965

Stations closed	Date
Ynyslas †††	14 June 1965
Llandre ††††	14 June 1965
Bow Street	14 June 1965

* Replaced by a new station adjacent to the old one.

** These opened as temporary stations on 17 January 1994 during bridge strengthening work.

*** Replaced by the Cambrian station about 1,000 yards to the west.

**** This was a private halt - it was known as Scafell Cutting until May 1876 when it became Scafell. It closed in July 1891 and reopened as Scafell Halt in July 1913.

† Known as Caersws until 3 January 1863.

†† Known as Glandovey until 1 July 1904.

††† Known as Ynys-las in early days but had been renamed by 1878.

†††† Known as Llanfihangel until 1 August 1916.

Forden Station, scene of a collision on 26 November 1904.

Cambrian main line (Welshpool to Aberystwyth)

Montgomery Station, looking towards Machynlleth, 23 August 1954.

Cambrian main line (Welshpool to Aberystwyth)

An accident on the line near Talerddig, 18 January 1921.

CAMBRIAN RLYS. SMASH "TALERDDIG" JAN. 18. 1921.

Cambrian main line (Welshpool to Aberystwyth)

Llanbrynmair Station.

Cambrian main line (Welshpool to Aberystwyth)

Cemmes Road Station.

Cambrian main line (Welshpool to Aberystwyth)

Glandyfi Station.

Cambrian main line (Welshpool to Aberystwyth)

Bow Street Station, looking towards Machynlleth, 18 June 1963.

Cambrian main line (Welshpool to Aberystwyth)

GWR/LNWR joint line (Shrewsbury to Welshpool)

Station   *Date of closure*
Breidden *   12 September 1960

* Known as Middletown until 1 June 1919 and Middletown Hills until 1 February 1928.

Middletown (later Breidden) Station.

Wolf's Castle Halt, looking towards Fishguard, 8 July 1958.

GWR main line to Fishguard

Station	Date of closure
Wolf's Castle Halt	6 April 1964
Welsh Hook Halt	6 April 1964
Mathry Road *	6 April 1964
Jordanston Halt	6 April 1964
Fishguard & Goodwick **	September 1972

* Known as Mathry until 7 July 1924.

** Known as Goodwick until 1 May 1904; it closed in 1964 only to reopen in 1965.